What HINDUS Can Do

What HINDUS Can Do

D.C. Nath, IPS (Retd.)

Manas Publications
(We Convert Fighters into Writers)
New Delhi-110002 (INDIA)

MANAS PUBLICATIONS
(We Convert Fighters into Writers)
(Publishers - Library Suppliers - Importers & Exporters)
4402/5-A, Ansari Road (Opp. HDFC Bank)
Darya Ganj, New Delhi - 110 002 (India)
Off.: 011-40198110, Fax: 011-23272766
E-mail : manaspublications@gmail.com
manaspub6@gmail.com

2nd Impression 2026 (FP - 2017)

ISBN : 978-81-7049-529-1

₹ 395/-

Designed by
Manas Publications

Printed in India at
R.K. Print Services, Delhi

Published by Mrs Suman Lata for
Manas Publications
4402/5-A, Ansari Road (Opp HDFC Bank),
Darya Ganj, New Delhi - 110 002 (INDIA)

Dedication

This is my sincere call to the vibrant youth of the Motherland to save Her in this time of crisis. This is my humble prayer to the mothers to guide them to fulfill their mission. Their mission, in the language of the toughest water sport, namely rowing, should be to "die on the boat". And, Oh, Mother! Bless us all to serve you till we breathe our last.

"Vandemataram"

Acknowledgement

It will be only too correct on my part to duly acknowledge my sincere debt to my senior colleagues and other friends, from whose thoughts I have borrowed freely indeed. There are too many to name them. First, my sincere debt to Shri J.P. Sharma for having so kindly written the excellent **"<u>Foreword</u>"**, putting across very precisely the crux of the problems facing the Hindus. Then, my respectful regards to my scholar friend Shri R.K. Ohri, who had taken the trouble of correcting my mistakes and offering suggestions. His fine and deft touches have tremendously embellished the quality of my submission. I also take this opportunity to acknowledge the support and inspiration from Shri D.K. Mittal, a very low-profile and scholar friend of mine.

And in these days of internet, a perennial source of learning, I would also like to acknowledge my indebtedness to all those friends, from whose mails I grafted whatever suited my thesis. It has not been possible to quote them all in the Note, primarily because that at times affect the flow of reading. Besides, they are too many and hence I dare not attempt to mention names of all, lest I offend those whom I might have failed to name inadvertently. Nevertheless, I must go on record I received a lot of help and derived inspirations from the writings of the noted political commentators

Dr. S. Gurumurthy, Dr. Subramanian Swamy, Dr. A.P. Joshi, Hiranmay Karlekar, Ramtanu Moitra, Dr. S. Kalyanaraman, Dr. Gautan Sen, Dr. K.V. Paliwal, T.A. Chari, V.S. Sundaram, Ramashray Upadhyay, Priyadarshi Dutta, Jitendra Khurana and Shankarendu Datta Majumdar. My special thanks to Shankarendu, who not only went through the script very carefully, virtually edited it and made some useful suggestions as well. Newspapers and periodicals have been great sources of information that I must also acknowledge.

I will like to go on record to sincerely appreciate Shri Sanjit Kanwar and Uma for their executive assistance. But for Uma's patience in deciphering my scribbling and typing these out neatly, this publication would not have seen the light of the day whatsoever.

Then, my debt to the publisher-friend Manas Publications, but for whose running about I would have been nowhere near completing this piece.

And finally, I bow to the Eternal Mother for having constantly goading and guiding me literally all through.

Foreword

How would the Hindus of India react if told that Hinduism may become extinct in India in another 40/50 years. According to one observer, a majority including the secularists, will dismiss the prediction as being of no consequence. Another section will question its plausibility on the ground of Hinduism having survived in India for over five thousand years in spite of all odds. There will be only a few who will pause to consider the matter seriously and proceed to examine the threats and to consider what can be done to avoid the catastrophe.

What are the major threats making the outlook for Hinduism so bleak? These are both external and internal. Two comparatively young convert-seeking religions – Islam and Christianity, which had been largely unsuccessful in their attempts to conquer India for Allah and Jesus respectively during the periods when India was ruled by their followers, have been making much better headway in the post 1947 India. [For details of the Christian effort see—**(1) "Preparing for the Harvest" by V K Shashikumar in Tehelka magazine and (2) "Breaking India" by Rajeev Malhotra and Arvindam Neelakandan; and for the Islamic Jihad, see (a) "The Long March Of Islam" and (b) "The Bell Tolls for a Truncated India", both by R K Ohri]**

What has contributed very significantly to the recent rapid strides made by evangelism in India is the presence of thousands and thousands of NGOs with staff presence in all parts of India and massive funding by the international Christian network. The presence of a Roman Catholic as the ultimate repository of Government power for a long time had been no small advantage. Islamic Jihad, on the other hand, is surging ahead also on the strength of its demography, the fervour of its followers, and the electoral power of the Muslim votes. And like the Christians, Islamists in India is also the beneficiary of financial and logistics inputs from Pakistan and the Middle East. Several researchers have written about how the behaviour of Muslim minorities becomes more and more demanding and threatening as their share in the population increases.

Facilitating the progress of Christianity and Islam is the democratic system of government followed in India. In spite of the Hindus constituting about 80% of the population, state power was for long in a combination of Christians and Muslims, supported by some "nominal" Hindus who seem to have no regard for their religion or its followers. That coterie had worked out a formula for winning elections, according to which the combined votes of Muslims+Christians + votes of the so called secular Hindus were enough to give them a majority of seats in Parliament. The assumption is that the Christians and the Muslims voting together as a block will prevail over the nominally more numerous Hindus because the Hindus are hopelessly divided into factions and vote only as members of the caste, and regional or linguistic or other groups to which they may happen to belong, thus frittering away the advantage of their numerical superiority.

To strengthen their vote bank, the erstwhile ruling dispensation had resorted to a massive illegality by dividing the population of India into two groups. Starting with the former Prime Minister's declaration in Dec, 2006, that 'the minorities, particularly the Muslims have the first claim on the nation's resources', the UPA II government had divided the population of India into two groups (1) the religious minorities-Muslims Christians, Sikhs, Buddhists and Parsis and (2) the Hindus. Huge favours amounting to several thousand crores of rupees had been granted to the first group for facilitating their progress in the fields of education, employment and economic advancement. The details of such favours may be seen by visiting the website of the **Ministry of Minority Affairs**.

The favours granted to the religious minorities were unwarranted, inequitable and blatantly violative of the provisions of the Constitution of India. In the first place, they violate the Constitutional guarantee that the state shall not discriminate against any citizen on the ground of caste, creed etc. Secondly, they are against the principles of equity and natural justice in as much as they give huge privileges and financial favours to some classes and deprive the Hindus of the same favours only and only on the ground of religion. Serious research has proved that the four religious minorities viz Christians, Sikhs, Buddhists and Parsis are much better off than the Hindus in all the globally recognized human development indicators. It is, therefore, obvious that the favours granted to the minorities have not been granted with the objective of relieving poverty or any other kind of backwardness. These are nothing except a bribe for their votes.

There are also some painful reminders of Hindu poverty. The almost exclusive Hindu presence among the roadside beggars in large towns, the high proportion of Hindu farmers committing suicides, and the number of Hindu parents selling their children to escape the pangs of hunger are visible signs of Hindu poverty. Rural incomes being substantially lower than urban incomes, it is axiomatic that the 74% Hindus living in rural areas and largely pursuing low income professions include substantial numbers of those stricken by abject poverty. Denying them the means of improving their lot is virtually condemning them and their future generations to a life of grinding poverty, poor health and without hope of a better future as also perhaps forcing them to improve their lot by converting to any of the favoured religions.

Hindus will be committing suicide if they continue the policy of doing nothing to save themselves. But before doing anything, they must understand their present perilous situation and the stark future facing them. Once they do that, the first and immediate step must be to sink their differences and to unite to claim their rightful share in the state power. Another step which must be taken immediately is to challenge the unconstitutional and discriminatory actions of the Central and state governments in various courts of the country. They must get rid of the weaknesses that have crept into their religion. At present the situation is that the Hindus have little knowledge of their own religion and virtually none of the competing religions. Once they get to know the heights attained by ancient Hindus in almost every field of human endeavour and the contribution made to the development of human civilization, they will start taking pride in their religion and be prepared to defend it

Shri D C Nath, President of the Patriots Forum, is one of the few Hindus who have given much serious thought to the problem .The ideas contained in his book titled **'What The Hindus Can Do'** need to be studied and acted upon by every Hindu interested in the survival of Hinduism.

J P Sharma
Vice President,
Patriots' Forum

New Delhi,

Letter From Shri R.K. Ohri

Dear Dhanesh,

As desired by you, I have read, re-read and suggested some additions/alterations in your fabulously candid book. Kudos to you for deciding to return to the facile power of your pen! You have brilliant ideas and commitment to Mother India which you must keep going by writing oftener.

The additions proposed by me have been highlighted in yellow pencil. As an author, you have the liberty to omit whatever you don't want to state in your essay.

By this opportunity may I suggest that you may persuade VIF to organise a seminar - or at least a no-holds-barred brain-storming session on the subject?
Pl. ack receipt of the document.

Warm regards.
Ram

Summary of Action Points

- Know Yourself
- Take Pride And Cultivate Love For The Motherland
- Urgent Need To Revisit The Past
- Unlearn And Learn History
- We Hindus Are A Nation
- Know The Lessons Of History
- Know Your Religion
- Hindu-Sikh Unity A Must
- Fight And Remove Stigma Of Being Communal
- Primary Duty Of The Hindus
- Guard Against Threat/Temptation Of Conversion
- Invoke Women Power/'Stree Shakti'
- Hindus Need To Unite
- Arouse The Hindu Middle Class Intelligentsia
- Tickle The Hindu Lawyers
- Appeal To The Hindu Youth
- Need To Expose Bitter Truth
- Fight To Prevent Corruption
- Know The Dangers
- Know Facts About Fast-Paced Communal Divide
- Need To Fight The Proposed Prevention Of Communal Violence Bill
- Learn Some Lessons From Muzaffarnagar Riots
- Know The Muslim Mind

An Explanation

It was proposed to bring this out as a monograph in late 2013.I had sent the draft two senior colleagues. One of them (Shri R K Ohri) had deeply scrutinized the piece and gave some excellent suggestions for improvement and also made one or two critical corrections. On his suggestion, Shri J P Sharma even graciously wrote the Introduction.

I have tried to put things in brief just to impress upon the Hindus what they can do for the country. It is not a piece of research work. It is a summation of thoughts gathered over the years. The subjects are such on most of which separate and independent books can be written.

After having stirred up the hornet's nest by writing a piece on: **"It is a Sin to be a Hindu in India"** (copy placed at the end), I thought it was incumbent on me to try and suggest some practical and implementable suggestions on what should be or could be done to retrieve the situation or rather to reverse the situation. That is why the title "**What The Hindus Can Do**". Even though it may lead to some uncertain or ambiguous speculation or may even put off some readers against proceeding further, the choice of the title is deliberate. It was the result of deep thought and was arrived at after serious consultations with learned as well as commoner friends.

The first question is: **<u>Who is a Hindu?</u>** A Hindu is a citizen of Hindusthan or Bharatvarsh In any case, we do not have to go far. Let us straightaway turn to **<u>Swami Vivekananda</u>.** "Then and then alone you are a Hindu when the very name Hindu sends through you a galvanic shock of strength. Then and then you are a Hindu when every man and woman who bears the name Hindu, from any country, speaking our language or any other language, becomes at once the nearest and dearest to you. Then alone you are a Hindu when the distress of anyone bearing the name Hindu comes to your heart and makes you feel as if your son or daughter were in distress".

Swamiji, called upon Hindus to take pride in being a Hindu: "When a man has begun to be ashamed of his ancestors, the end has come. Here am I, one of the least of the Hindu race yet proud of my race, proud of my ancestors. I am proud to call myself a Hindu. I am proud that I am one of your unworthy servants. I am proud that I am a countryman of yours, you the descendants of the sages, you the descendants of the most glorious Rishis the world ever saw".

Coming to recent times, let us read what M C Chagla, an eminent jurist and a former Union Education Minister had to say about himself, "I am a Muslim by religion; but by culture and race, I am a Hindu".

> ***P.S.*** *(Article 25 (2) (b), Explanation II stipulates–insub-clause (b) of clause (2), the **<u>reference to Hindus</u>** shall be **<u>construed</u>** as including a reference to persons professing the Sikh, Jain or Buddhist religion, and the reference to Hindu religious institutions shall be construed accordingly).*

If, I myself as an individual, having gone through the full course of education from one of the best educational institutions in the country, nay, then in the world, in early fifties and having had the privilege of serving the country in some responsible official position and being a denizen of Bharatvarsha, drawing a healthy pension, feel shy to call myself a Hindu, fie on me and on and all those who would shy away from calling herself or himself a Hindu, a proud Hindu at that for fear of being called communal by so-called and ill-educated "secularists". We should have the mental courage to declare ourselves "proud Hindus" from every roof-top. And, we should also teach our children, all members of the family, to do so with legitimate pride. Here is a case where we alone can help ourselves.

The submission has, however, to be precise yet holistic and doable. I am keenly aware this "task" is beyond my capability. Also, keeping in mind how difficult it is these days to engage some one's attention for long, I had initially thought of adopting the method of putting my thoughts on the subject in the bullet-point format. But, then, I soon realised the subject discussed, even though treated in brief, will not lend itself to such technique. Every aspect in this piece, even though briefly scripted for the sake of ensuring brevity, but ensuring enough clarity, would possibly justify or call for a larger dissertation. It is neither a crime-thriller nor a romantic love-story or on any excitable current topic, in which case a learned author, by virtue of his mastery of the language, can carry the readers with him.

I have, therefore, taken it as a challenge how to attract and retain the attention of the busy people, each tied to his or her own vocation. The little time they get for relaxation is either spent for the family or spent on entertaining T.V. serials or huffing and puffing 24X7 news channels, at times catering unsubstantiated stories, creating an artificial hype or even undue societal tension. In order to be able to engage their attention and offer them something "as from the fast-food centers", I have put a **"Summary of Action Points"**, just on top of the note. One in a hurry can glance through it, choose any one '**Action Point**' and then if anyone feels interested, she or he can look up any other item, though the '**Action Points**' have been put in some sequence or chain of thoughts. Thus, I have tried my best. Even then, my best can always be bettered. And imperfection can always be there. And, I am also keenly aware that the future belongs to the learner. There would hardly be anything new in my submission. I have just attempted juxtaposing facts so as to justify my contention. My simple purpose has been to share with the readers what I had gathered as a student, then during the course of service career, both in the government and later at the corporate sector, but more so, from the thoughts and ideas I could garner from interactions with some senior and learned colleagues in recent years. I have avoided statistical analysis, which at times appears complex or confusing. Also, my intention has never been to appear didactic. It has all through been a common sense and yet analytical approach. But, I value the truth and have faith in our civilisational ethos. So, I firmly stand by every statement made, statements based on facts and truth or authentic history.

Let us in this context clarify another point. Although some people may find fault with the presentation as carrying communal feelings, that is far from the truth, or, is downright on arrant nonsense. Such an observation, made only because of the title of the paper, will be a misinterpretation. **There has been no communal tinge** or prejudice at all. The sum-up in the concluding remarks will, we hope, clarify that.

A discerning reader may also find the presentation as somewhat biased. Yes, it is biased, biased towards or in defence of Indic civilisational ethos and that has been deliberate. It is for the esteemed readers to take this or reject it. There can be any negative pitfalls in every system, including Hinduism, such as, prevalence of superstition, Brahmanical tyranny etc. But these are aberrations, even distortions, e.g. the custom of sati which found prompt public acceptance because of barbaric invaders' penchant for carrying away Hindu women as booty.

In a nutshell, my attempt has been to project the positive aspects. That is, to tell the truth and nothing but the truth. There can also be omissions of some vital aspects. Those may be counted as my failures. But, unwittingly if some factual mistakes have crept in, I will feel honoured to be made aware of such lapses. That will be my education, another stage of learning, and I shall feel obliged. If nothing else, that will be a proof that you had taken the trouble of reading my frankspeak. That will be a great reward for me. Let me again emphasise at the end, we do not carry any hatred or malice against any non-Hindus. Our religious culture and civilisational ethos do not endorse that at all.

The **guiding motto** has been: even if not fully, that the future of the majority population in this holy land of **Bharatvarsh**, namely, the Hindus, lies, to a large extent, in their own hands. There is no point in blaming others, more so the State authority, which is the easiest thing to do. I humbly and strongly believe there is scope for doing much more on our part to rectify or ameliorate the distress quite effectively if we think and act, both individually and collectively. This is what I have tried to project all through and stage by stage. As it happens in many historical processes, time is not on our side. So, there is need for urgency in our thoughts and actions. It is not for nothing, therefore, the aphorism goes, **"God Helps Those Who Help Themselves"**. So, the Hindus will have to help themselves. It is worth remembering what the British philosopher writer Joseph Konrad has written in the preface to **Earnest Hemmingway's** noted book, **"For Whom The Bell Tolls": "Never Try to Know For Whom The Bell Tolls: It Tolls for Thee"**. Hence, this self-introspection.

Perhaps, I have overshot my original objective but then ideas and inspirations came by and by and I incorporated those, hoping the presentation will be self-contained. It is, however, difficult to assess one's own faults. All of us are mere mortals.

Then, a **request**. In case you feel convinced about my submission and if it leads to some creative and enlightened discussion, kindly share it with friends and friends of friends, as I am fond of saying.

I sincerely hope, my submission, even if not proving helpful, will provoke some readers to react and add to carry forward what I would fondly believe to be an on-going debate or discourse, whatever one would like to call it. That will be my reward. Not responding to my thoughts would be a dampener.

New Delhi
2013.

(D.C. Nath)

What The Hindus Can Do (An Introspection)

Even though ill-equipped, I have taken courage in both hands to undertake this exercise with the hope and belief it will lead our compatriots to think what can really be done Hindus to protect ourselves against the odds being faced during day-to-day living or even against the much-dreaded "civilizational threats", if one may like to put it that way. I ... over whether we could have used ... "Must Do" instead of "Can Do" ... would have been rather audacious ... case, to begin from the beginning.

Know Yourself

* Though it may sound theoretical, ... foremost requirement is "Know Your... Proud of Your Past". In the wor... prophet of India, Swami Vivekan... accepted as the progenitor of India's ... movement, "Out of the past ... Look back, therefore, as far as ... of the eternal fountains that are ... that, look forward, march forward ... brighter, greater, much higher than ...

What The Hindus Can Do (An Introspection)

Even though ill-equipped, I have taken courage in both hands to undertake this exercise with the hope and belief it will lead our compatriots to think what can really be done Hindus to protect ourselves against the odds being faced during day-to-day living or even against the much-dreaded "civilisational threats", if one may like to put it that way. I had deeply thought over whether we could have used the expression "**Must Do**" instead of "**Can Do**", but then felt that would have been rather audacious on my part. In any case, to begin from the beginning.

Know Yourself:

- Though it may sound theoretical, the first and foremost requirement is: "**Know Yourself**" and "**Feel Proud of Your Past**". In the words of the "**warrior prophet**" of India, **Swami Vivekananda**, universally accepted as the progenitor of India's national freedom movement, "**Out of the past is built the future. Look back, therefore, as far as you can, drink deep of the eternal fountains that are behind, and after that, look forward, march forward and make India brighter, greater, much higher than she ever was.**"

This feet-on-the ground patriot saint, who was almost blindly proud of his past and was rather contemptuous of so-called scholars unduly critical of India's history, had, therefore, also said, "**Say not one harsh word against this society. I love it for its past greatness**." These observations, made in the last decade of the 19th century, holds good even today. For those who would not remember or may not have known, this is what the globally famous historian **Will Durant** had said:

"India: The Mother of All": "India was the motherland of our race, and Sanskrit the Mother of Europe's all languages. India was the Mother of our philosophy, of much of our mathematics, of the ideals embodied in Christianity of self-government and democracy.

"In many ways, Mother India is the Mother of all of us".

Another great British historian E.P. Thompson famously said: "All the convergent influences of the world, Hindu, Muslim, Christian, Secular, Stalinist, Liberal, Maoist, Democratic Socialist, Gandhian run through India. There is not a single thought that is being thought in the West or the East that is not active in some Indian mind".

We may also note at this stage what the greatest historian of the last century Arnold Toynbee had said about the Indian civilisational values. "It is already becoming clear that a chapter which had a Western beginning (?) will have to have an Indian ending if it is not to end in the destruction of the human race. At this

supremely dangerous moment in human history, the only way of salvation for mankind is the Indian way- Emperor Ashoka's and Mahatma Gandhi's principle of non-violence and Sri Ramakrishna's testimony to the harmony of religions. Here we have an attitude and spirit that make it possible for the human race to grow together into a single family-and, in the Atomic age, this is the only alternative to destroying ourselves". We have deliberately refrained from referring to Max Muller because he has been termed as an Indophile, though not correctly.

Here is, however, another specific illustration of India's civilisational spread. In his treatise on civilisational encounters, **Swami Vivekananda** exultingly wrote how Lord Shiva on his bull and with his "domoru", travelled from India, on the one side, to Sumatra, Borneo, Celebes, Australia, as far as the shores of America". "Mother Kali", the Swami continued "charting the spread of Hinduism", is still exacting her worship in China and Japan". Hu Shin, one of the best known Chinese scholar-diplomats and one of the legendary leaders of Chinese thought, had exclaimed, "*China was overwhelmed, baffled and overjoyed. She begged and borrowed from this munificent giver (India). China's indebtedness to India can never be fully told*".

Well, some very useful thoughts and facts have been thrown up on this ticklish issue. When seized of the matter in 2006, after the publication of that tome, namely, **The Religious Demography of India**, the Rashtriya Swamsevak Sangha (RSS) had proclaimed that in future all Hindus should have three children (like in Australia- one for the father, one for the mother and one for the country). The Malthusian theory, propagated by the Britishers, is believed to have been a subturefuge to keep the native population under check, was the view from another. Yet another serious thinker believes without adopting an "aggressive population policy", the Hindus will not realise the danger or wake up to the danger of being physically overrun by the Christian-Muslim combo. Yet, another sensitive writer wants all the Dharma Acharyas to issue injunction against birth control measures by the Hindus (may be just like the Roman Catholics). Getting to realities with the present day norms being followed by the Hindus, there would not have been no Lord Krishna and no Rabindranath Tagore, both of whom were the eighth child of their respective & revered parents.

And, we have no right to disinherit them.

Here we feel tempted to quote the beautiful and highly relevant stanzas from two different British poets.

A Psalm of Life - By Henry Wadsworth Longfellow

Tell me not, in mournful numbers,
Life is but an empty dream!
For the soul is dead that slumbers,
And things are not what they seem.

Life is real! Life is earnest!
And the grave is not its goal;
Dust thou art, to dust returnest,
Was not spoken of the soul.

Not enjoyment, and not sorrow,
Is our destined end or way;
But to act, that each to-morrow
Find us farther than to-day.

Art is long, and Time is fleeting,
And our hearts, though stout and brave,
Still, like muffled drums, are beating
Funeral marches to the grave.

In the world's broad field of battle,
In the bivouac of Life,
Be not like dumb, driven cattle!
Be a hero in the strife!

Trust no Future, howe'er pleasant!
Let the dead Past bury its dead!
Act,— act in the living Present!
Heart within, and God o'erhead!

Lives of great men all remind us
We can make our lives sublime,
And, departing, leave behind us
Footprints on the sands of time;

Footprints, that perhaps another,
Sailing o'er life's solemn main,
A forlorn and shipwrecked brother,
Seeing, shall take heart again.

Let us, then, be up and doing,
With a heart for any fate;
Still achieving, still pursuing,
Learn to labor and to wait.

Elegy Written in a Country Churchyard—By Thomas Gray

Full many a gem of purest ray serene,
The dark unfathom'd caves of ocean bear:
Full many a flow'r is born to blush unseen,
And waste its sweetness on the desert air.

Before we proceed further, let us again take note of what our **Yuga Purush Swami Vivekananda** had to say about the youth in the late the nineteenth century that holds good even today.

His call to the youth was: "This is the time to decide your future while you possess the energy of the youth, not when you are worn out and jaded, but in the freshness and vigour of youth: work, this is the time, for the flowers alone are to be laid at the fest of the Lord. Let this be our determination, and may he, the Lord, bless us and lead us to the fulfillment of our aims."

Let us all, therefore, **Take Pride and Cultivate Love For The Motherland**, just as we love our biological mother. It is said, and indeed, well said, that on getting up in the morning, one should touch the land and pray, "Oh, Mother, do let me have the opportunity to serve you better". To imbibe this spirit, one cannot do anything better than reading the classical text, incorporating the **Twenty Seven Lectures of Swami Vivekananda**, (**Colombo to Almora: The Twenty-Seven Lectures**" (Vijayanti Press, Madras).One can then perhaps turn a patriot overnight. Let us read this once and once again and feel the difference it brings to our personality and emotion, emotions turning in to love for the Motherland. In short, we will become true patriots, a "fierce patriot", unknowingly perhaps.

We can perhaps at this stage also turn to our sacred Shastras also. **Taitriya Upanishad** says, "**Revere your mother and father as Gods**". Bhishma Pitamaha says in Mahabharata, **"the father equals ten teachers. But the mother equals ten fathers or perhaps the whole world in importance"**. Unfortunately, reverence is missing in the modern society, says, **Paul Woodruff**, professor of philosophy and Dean at the Texas University (US) in his treatise "**Reverence: Revering a Forgotten virtue**".

Would we not, therefore, make renewed efforts to revise and intently cultivate this great virtue? That requires no outside help! Let all of us, therefore, try to inculcate love for the Motherland into all members of the family, especially the children. The test of our "**deshprem**" or love for the Motherland rests on the simple fact when we feel our heart bleed for her.

An Urgent Need To Revisit The Past:

There is, **An Urgent Need To Revisit The Past**: We, the Indians, the denizens of Hindustan (the Bharatvarsh of the Puranas), have forgotten our history and so we **Need to Revisit The Past,** as the historians in the West have done in revisiting the Greek and Roman mythology with the help of archaeology, geology and other connected branches of science. The readers may in this connection refer to the writer's highly acclaimed brief presentation on "**Revisiting the Future of India**", (available on CD). Special mention in this connection needs to be made of a superb collation by **<u>Sudhir Birodkar</u>**, "**<u>India's Contribution to World Culture</u>**" (this was also available on the internet) in that presentation. If nothing else, a simple perusal of that presentation, will make today's youth feel proud as an Indian, a Bharatvashi, a supreme need of the hour. That generates self confidence.

Unlearn and Learn History:

<u>Unlearn and Learn History</u>: It is not without truth it is often said the Indians do not have a sense of history or do not know the art or science of writing history. Not much details of India's hoary past were available from Indian sources or scriptures. Most of us till the fifties of the 20th century, were taught history through books, written by the Britishers or from what had been chronicled by foreign visitors, including Muslim traders. And then, there had been a Marxist school of thought, interpreting history through their own coloured lens. The first authentic attempt to write India's history was through the Bharatiya Vidya Bhawan series, initiated by K.M. Munshi and edited by R.C. Majumdar, inthe beginning in late or mid-fifties of the last century. It will be worth briefly noting at this stage that thanks to scientific research and painstaking work for three years, two Chennai-based botanists have literally proved that the story of Lord Rama, generally believed to be mythical, was a true-life account. They started with the study of fauna and fora at Ayodhya and then ultimately reached Sri Lanka, traversing the route described by Rishi Valmiki, physically identified and verified on the ground all places en route followed by Lord Rama, Laxman and Sita to Sri Lanka (**ref. Plant and Animal Diversity in Valmiki Ramayana by Amrithalingam and Sudhakar**). It is, therefore, not without reason, a case has also been filed against the Government of India's deliberate attempt to destroy the Ram Setu, which too is a physical reality, as archaeologists and the Experts Committee set up on this have declared. Incidentally, only the other day, the Sri Lankan Government have also expressed their concern to the Government of India over the proposed Ram Sethu project.

We Hindus Are a Nation

Let us here take note of the fact, not generally taught to us and not known to many either, that **'We Hindus Are a Nation'** from time immemorial. The fact that **'We Hindus Are A Nation'** is by no means a new idea. This idea has been with us from the dawn of history. Without going into the hoary past, let us trace it from the latter half of the 19th century. If we read the writings of **Swami Dayanand Saraswati** (1824-1883) of Arya Samaj, we can see the underlying notion that **'We Hindus Are A Nation'**. We can see the same refrain in the writings of **Bankim Chandra Chattopadhyay** (1838-1894) of **Vande Mataram** fame and **Sri Aurobindo** (1872-1950). In their writings, we find a clear and confident assertion that **'We Hindus Are A Nation'** and not just a religious community. The basic perception of **Vinayak Damodar Savarkar** (1883-1966) was also the same which he forcefully presented in his book **'Hindutva'**. However, the saint, sage and seer **Swami Vivekananda** made the most powerful pronouncement of this idea. Throughout his brief but momentous life, **Swami Vivekananda** proclaimed loudly, clearly and consistently the fact that **'We Hindus Are A Nation'**.

To this, we may also add what **Rishi Aurobindo** had said in 1909 in his now famous Uttarpura (West Bengal) speech: "India is identical with **'Sanatana Dharma'**. When therefore it is said that India shall rise, it is the **'Sanatana Dharma'** that shall rise. When it is said that India shall expand and extend itself, over the world. It is for the dharma and by the dharma that India exists. I say that it is the **'Sanatana Dharma'** which for us is nationalism."

Know The Lessons of History: Points To Quickly Learn:

i) That we had a hoary past or a full-blown **Akhand Bharat**, a thriving civilisation, now scientifically proved to be over 6000 years old;

ii) That the residents of 'Bharatvarsh' had a 'Chakraborti-rajan', (a sign of military valour), Chandragupta Maurya, the boundary of whose empire had extended at least up to Kandhar (Gandhar in Mahabharata) in the North/West. We had also adequate maritime power to have left indelible impressions in countries in the Far East, at least up to Indonesia, where the province of Bali is still a Hindu-majority area and the largest Hindu temple Angkor Vat is in Cambodia. One needs go across to nearby Bangkok to see almost-Hindu names, from arrival at the Kuala Lampur airport to the naming of posh hotels in the capital city. So, as we had said, we have forgotten our history and we will have to rediscover or relive our past;

iii) Thanks to a combination of general Indians' flavour for enterpreneurship, diligence, natural resources and maritime prowess, India was indeed a very rich country, attracting raiders from time to time and even in recent times, leading to great trade rivalry between the Britishers, the French and the Portuguese in establishing their footholds all along the coastal areas;

iv) That India, by all internationally accepted records, including from Muslim writers, has been the most severely ravaged, looted country and had suffered most in terms of mass killing, rape and all forms of torture at the hands of Muslim invaders over the centuries is known. Facts on these have all been duly chronicled and are available. In the language of <u>Will Durant</u> again: **"The Mohanmedan aggression (on India) is the bloodiest in history. It is a discouraging tale, for its evident moral is that civilization is a precious good, whose delicate complex order and freedom can at any moment be overthrown by barbarians invading from without and multiplying from within."** India has survived all that and also the more civilized looting by the British traders who later came to rule the country for over 200 years. The Britishers had deliberately distorted her history destroyed India's sound education system (reference Lord

Thomas Babington Macaulay's 'famous' Minute on Indian Education, Feb, 1838) and permanently sowed the seeds of Hindu-Muslim discord. It is worth quoting here what a known British journalist had observed, "The most effective way to destroy the people is to deny and obliterate their own understanding of their history", The one thing, however, the Britishers, could not, do is to change the intrinsically democratic ethos (the highest example of Lord Rama banishing his wife Sita Devi following peoples' wish- "**raj tantra is praja tantra**" or "**rajdharma is people's wish**") and the basic resilience of the Indic civilisation, primarily because of its inherent culture of assimilation and tolerance. We shall dilate on this aspect later.

v) However, despite all the torture, savagery, killing, looting, etc., the Muslim raiders, and even about 1000 year old Muslim rule over India, they never succeeded in subjugating or supplanting the Indian civilisation. In other words, it was not a "civilisational conquest". Despite having undergone the worst of human miseries, the Hindus had never surrendered. They rebuilt and were overrun but, they rose again and again. That has been the story of Hindu resistance. It has been the march of unbroken civilisational history and unprecedented also. On the other hand, a good number of foreign Muslims finally settled down and found home under the umbrella of the Indic civilization. The problem of the Indians (then all Hindus) was that despite having spread the Indian culture, they were in some ways rather insular in terms of knowledge or rules of warfare. The shastras taught them to be moral and correct even when fighting. They hardly "knew their enemy", which, as taught by the Chinese strategist Sun Tsu, world have meant winning half the battle;

vi) It will, however, be a misreading of history to believe that independence was won through non-violence only. The early leaders of the nationalist movement, (termed as "terrorist" movement by the Britishers), then led by heroic people like "Masterda" (Surya Sen) of Chittagong Armoury Raid, who had set up the first Provisional Revolutionary Govt. of Independent India, did indeed stage an armed struggle. It would be knowledge to many that even the great preacher of co-existence on the principles of love, harmony and assimilation as learnt from Ramakrishna, Swami Vivekananda, according to his younger brother (Bhupendra Nata Dutta), who called him "Patriot Prophet", had recorded, he (Swami Vivekananda), determined to get rid of colonial subjugation, wanted to form a group of dedicated Sanyasis who could, if necessary, be prepared to launch an armed insurrection to win freedom", (Samit Kar, The Letters to the Editor, The Statesman, January 15, 2014). Though Mahatma Gandhi later led the nationalist movement through 'ahimsa', we must in the same breath recall that Netaji Subhas Chandra Bose had shaken the Brithishers by launching the Provisional Indian Govt. from Singapore through outright armed struggle. The last straw on the British authority was the naval mutiny at the Bombay dockyard.

Know Your Religion:

This was in tune with our religion-a religion that combines the wisdom of sages over the years and is not the result of any "revelation" by an individual, thrust on his followers. Leaving aside the theological part, Hinduism preaches compassion to all living beings, tolerance, assimilation, and synthesis. Vedas, which form the basis of Bhagavad Gita, Yoga Darshan and Upanishads, asks us to be simple **"Humans"** (Manurbhava), to be tolerant of others, to strive for unity and brotherhood. There is no concept of or an agenda for conversion in Vedas. So has it been beautifully stated "Let's bring Vedas to every door step. Let's bring Vedas to every human". Well, it is indeed worth reading the full text in http://agniveer.com/why-i-love-vedas-part-2/. Alongside, it also teaches how to disagree through arguments, etc. **'Tarkashastra'**, i.e, "**Vimarsh**" is a great science in Hinduism. Rishis like Paramhansa Ramakrishna also taught, 'jata mat, tata path', i.e., "as many views, so many paths". Dissonance is a part of our culture. The Noble Laureate **Amartya Sen** has spoken about "**The Argumentative Indian**". One can recall, Lord Krishna had urged Arjuna to pick up arms even against his grandfather Bhishma Pitamaha and Guru Dronacharya because it was his duty to protect dharma. This, in simple interpretation, means there is no place for cowardice while the question comes for protecting one's own dharma.

As a matter of fact, the very revered book "**Durga Saptashati**" contains a good deal of details of bloodshed and Hindu view of warfare. That is why we are misled when taught, "**Ahimsa parama dharma**". That is the half truth. The full sloka includes: "**dharma himsa tathai vacha**", that is, taking up arms when needed is also an act of dharma. One can, therefore, see all Hindu gods and goddesses are armed. Durgashakti was invoked to demolish Asura, the demon. So, not to defend oneself against adharma is no virtue, rather is a downright failure or cowardice. One could also take note in this connection of what is known or used to be taught as **"Shastra Pujan".** That is why we see in epics like the Mahabharata how different warriors used to offer puja or respectful homage to their weapons. The example of Arjuna worshipping that "Shiv Dhanush" before picking that up or Lord Krishna in Ramayan doing the same as a boy in the court of Kansa. It may also be recalled **Swami Vivekananda** had advised the youth that they would reach God earlier with better biceps than reading the Gita. Weak body leads to weaker mind and "weaker resolve". We must at least learn to protest and make that taken note of. We can and must fight for our rights by legal means. We are much too much on the quieter side and unduly tolerant even in justifiable cases when it becomes very necessary to make our perception and intention clear to those concerned. There needs be no resort to any surreptitious means. The truth does prevail though at times it does not appear so but it will prevail in the long run even in these days of Kaliyuga.

All these are stated not to preach militancy or violence but to simply remind or urge ourselves to follow the teachings with examples in our Shastras forming the religion. So, let us know our own religion, perform the duties, as enjoined on us, and not go on complaining or moaning over what others are doing, against us, etc. In simple words, be a crusader for the Hindu faith, without being fussy about the rituals that are very often being misused against us. To put it in another way, there is an undiluted need for bringing about the much-needed Hindu unity, discussed later in this note. It may be worth noting in passing here that while our knowledge, at least for the majority of us, of the Vedas is practically nil, markets are getting flooded with books on Vedas by foreign writers. So, has it been said, **"Revive Vedas in India before their teachings/ metaphysics reach Bharat from US/Europe".** There could be indeed a drive to revive Vedas in regional languages also.

A word of caution! Yes, "religion and religion alone" has been the corner-stone of the Indian civilization. **Swami Vivekananda** had assessed, the raison d'etre for the nation's survival against foreign oppression was: it held on "to God, to the treasure-house of religion and spirituality". It is its strength but can turn into a dangerous source of weakness as well if dogmatism or bigotry takes over. We must not cling to worn-out or imposed rituals. There have, therefore, been any number of reformers like Ramanujam, Sankara, Nanak, Chaitanya and Kabir to ensure we remain in tune, without losing cultural moorings, with the demands of the changing times.

Hindu-Sikh Unity A Must

Hindus and Sikhs are in real terms more than "blood-brothers". Guru Govind Singh had asked every family (obviously then the majority Hindu families) to give their first child to him in defence of the country against the marauders and thus was formed the Sikh strength. Many devout Sikh as well as Hindu friends are unaware of this basic truth. Unfortunately some divisive politicians have created an atmosphere of distrust between these two "blood-brothers". The notorious anti-Sikh riots of 1984 were planned and executed by politicians to break up the unity of Hindu-Sikh fraternity. In order to do justice to this basic issue, I take this opportunity to quote from a scholar-friend with Sikh lineage: 'First and foremost, Sikhism is nothing but a militarised version of Hinduism. Guru Govind Singh was not only very well-versed in Sanskrit, he was a true worshiper of Chandi Devi (i.e, Maa Durga) and Lord Shiva. In "Bichitra Natak", he explained that "Guru Panth" is an extension of Sri Ram's dynasty and that Guru Nanak was a direct descendant of Kush (son of Sri Ram) while he himself was a direct descendant of another son of Sri Ram, Lava".

It is, therefore, not for noting that the noted Sikh scholar **Khushwant Singh**, who has written the most authentic history of Sikhs, in two volumes, had observed "Sikhism is the purest form of Vedanta". It may also be proper quote what Guru Nanak Dev has said in The **"Adi Granth Sahib", "Ved, Kitab kaho mat jhoot, jhoota who jo na vichare", Do not say that the Vedas and the other scriptures** are not true scriptures; **the**

individual who does not study them is an untruthful person". No wonder, therefore, **Swami Vivekananda** had also proclaimed: "Mark my words, every one of you will have to be Guru Govind Singh, if you want to do good to your country". Unfortunately, due to dirty politics and unfriendly circumstances, very few Sikh friends as well as Hindus are aware of this basic truth of traditional Hindu-Sikh fraternity. Mistakes on the part of a few Hindu religious leaders had also helped create some uncalled for hiatus between these two communities.

The nation owes its debt to the brave-heart Sikh brothers for the starling role they had played and have been playing in the defence of the country over the ages. They have etched out a distinct place for themselves in the history of India by virtue of their intense religious convictions and sacrifice for the nation based on unwavering nationalist spirit. But for these exemplary sacrifices in the past in defending the borders of Hindustan, there would not possibly have been either the Hindus or the Hindusthan, so asserts a scholar. Special kudos to the Sikh brothers, sisters and mothers from the rest of us all.

However, the truth that Hindus and Sikhs are "blood-brothers" will have to be re-established permanently for the sake of educating the vast multitude of ignorants who are not fully aware of the genesis and finer nuances of the Sikh history. And in the not-too-distant-past during the calamity called the partition, millions of Hindus and Sikhs came travelling together from Pakistan, trudging on foot, in carriages and carts to Hindusthan, now called **Bharatvarsh**.

Fight for Ensuring Universal Education/ Educate the Poor

An enabling factor for this would be to ensure universal education. The majority community could extend necessary cooperation to the government at various levels. Let us make it incumbent on all of us to bring up one poor illiterate individual--he or she—to the level of being called on educated Indian. This social malaise had actually been clearly identified by **Swamiji** as the late back as 1890s. He was quite clear, "**if the poor cannot come to education, education must go to him**". The full statement reads: "A nation is advanced in proportion as education and intelligence spread among the masses. The chief cause of India's ruin has been the monopolizing of the whole education and intelligence of the land, by dint of pride and royal authority, among a handful of men. If we are to rise again, we shall have to do it in the same way, i.e. by spreading education among the masses." He knew the hurdle too. "The great difficulty in the way of educating the poor [in India] is that the poor boys would rather help their fathers in the fields, or otherwise try to make a living, than come to the school... if the poor boy cannot come to education, education must go to him."

Need For Correct Reading & Learning: Sanskrit

Such distortions or lack of correct reading of history can and do at times even affect the psyche of the people in many ways. There has, therefore, to be correct reading and learning of some essential facts that go to shape the character of the nation. Most of us have forgotten that **Sanskrit**, the **Mother** of **All Languages**, formed the base of our cultural history & background. It is **a language that goes beyond words,** so has been beautifully written by Provashi Barun in the Hindustan Times, November 5, 2013. There is more to Sanskrit besides being the language of traditional Hindu worship, so observed another scholar Prof. (Dr.) Satyamurti of Delhi University. Do we, therefore not make some effort to revive this mother of all languages in its 'hometown' so to say? The 'secular', (under incorrect interpretation) government will not bother about it. So, it falls on the shoulders of hewers of wood and drawers of water to do whatever is required in this direction.

Since we are now in the mould of accepting our own inventions/discoveries only after those having received recognition from outside, let us note a few examples:

i. A Chair for Sanskrit was instituted at the University of Rome as early as 1891.
ii. **Sanskrit chanting** is in vogue in the **MIT Harvard**, since some years now;
iii. Students in Iowa (USA) University were engaged in enrolling for Sanskrit courses, especially those who practise yoga;
iv. According to Forbes **Magazine**, Sanskrit is the most suitable language for computer software.

As a matter of fact, given the sheer efficacy, both in classical and contemporary context, Universities outside India (some in India as well) are now engaged in improving the existing traditions of teaching Sanskrit (Provashi Barun).

The task involved may not in reality be that difficult over a period of time, particularly because the vocabulary of most of the prominent Indian languages, both in the South & the North, contains a large number of Sanskrit words. We have a village in Madhya Pradesh, where all residents converse only in Sanskrit. Swami Vivekananda, who was persistent that Sanskrit must be widely taught for fostering Indian identify (and possibly for unity as well). Dr. Subrahmaniyan Swamy in his key note address at the 150th birthday celebrations of Swami Vivekananda, at Chicago, 2013, said, we should, therefore, have a commitment to "**re-throne Sanskrit**" as Hindustan's link language and ensure a steady Sanskritisation of Hindi vocabulary, especially in bulletin as used to be the case soon after Independence.

Fight And Remove Stigma of Being Communal

One primary need after **Knowing The Religion** is to make it abundantly clear that **true Hindus**, who swear by the tenets Vedanta and Upanishads, even unknowingly, **cannot be communal**. The Hindus do not need any lesson on secularism. Of all the religions in the world, Hinduism is the most secular faith. We Hindus have over the ages accommodated and assimilated people of other faiths & countries. There had not been or has ever been any case of forcible conversion in the course of the 6000 year-old Hindu civilisation.

It would be worth remembering in this context the Supreme Court's ruling some years back that it was sad to know that Hindutva is often projected as a communal word. The Supreme Court had observed "it was an error of law to proceed on the assumption that Hinduism per se predicts an attitude hostile to other than Hindu religion", recently quoted by Ram Jethmalani in the Sunday Guardian (November 24, 2013). One can also in this background recall Swamiji's teachings. Swamiji was a staunch Hindu by conviction and the flag-bearer of Hinduism before the entire world. But, no one can accuse him to be communal by any stretch of imagination. The lessons he learnt from his Master Ramakrishna would just not permit him to be communal whatsoever. Netaji Subhas Chandra Bose has explained that in detail. (quoted in the conclusion) We will do well to organise seminars and engage the leaders of other faiths into some public debate on this. No government in the country will do it. It is we the common men who will have to take this up as a challenge & demolish any misperception in this regard.

Primary Duty of The Hindus

Along with the need to know and learn one's religion, one primary duty of the Hindus would be to protect and preserve their places of religious worship like temples or mandirs or pithasthans. We have failed to do so over the ages but have not learnt any lessons. This was primarily so because we had not thought of such dangers and hence had not developed any mechanism to defend such holy places. There is indeed a lot to learn in this respect from Sikh brothers and Muslims friends.

One thing leads to another. Unlike the friends in other religious faiths, in which attendance to places of worship is at times mandatory, not many among the Hindus are fond of visiting temples except to pray for divine intervention in times of need or crisis in personal affairs. This 'fault', if one may so describe it that way, is compounded by the fact that for reasons of following the path of "secularism", we have no lessons on religious studies in the mainstream academic institutions in the country. And, thanks to that 'great' and true Britishman, Lord Macaulay, who had understood the strength of Hindu education system and culture as the corner-stone of the resilience of Hindu strength for continued survival, had advised complete demolition, nay, abolition of the indigenous and contemptuously called the 'native' system of education in India. Resultantly, we have today virtually religiously ignorant Hindus. This lack of knowledge of their own religion and history do at times make educated Indians appear small and feel inferior at international get-togethers where they are looked down upon for their 'little' or virtually no knowledge of their own country or religion as such. Whom do we blame this upon? Hopefully there are now some indications that the state machinery is going to gear up towards reviewing our academic curricular.

It was a piece of learning the other day in this connection that when some Muslim friends, who had gone for performing holy 'haj' to Mecca, had stated that they had come from India, the concerned religious teacher asserted that meant they were Hindus. Even when the Muslim friends from India vehemently asserted that they were Muslims, the religious teacher countered them, "all that is okay but since you have come from Hindustan, the land of Hindus, we treat you as Hindus"! Well, we have no comments to add on that.

Guard Against Threat/Temptation of Conversion

<u>**Guard Against Threat/Temptation of Conversion**</u>: Religious conversion introduced in India long back has, over the last half-a-century or so, reached a dangerous proportion because of apparent and deliberate plan behind. It is worth noting that Hinduism is the only religion that does not believe in proselytisation or preaching conversion, just in stark contrast with what the Christian & Islamic friends are taught by their religious scriptures or leaders. While the fast-growth of Muslim population comes to notice easily, the Christians are believed to have come up to 8% of the Indian population according to a serious student of the subject. Hindu political influence has been gone down in Tamilnadu and Kerala substantially and conversions to Christianity have surged vertically in Andhra Pradesh. Nagaland & Mizoram are already lost causes. The prodigious funding they receive from

outside is an open knowledge. While all these are going on, the "secular" governments in the Centre or in the States are blind to or silent on the march of these religious faiths by devious means including maligning the Hindu faith, by highlighting the "faultiness" of Hinduism and even offering financial help. One of their primary aims is to attack the casteism among the Hindus, without exposing that both the Christians and Muslims themselves have too many sects among themselves. The bitter fight between Protestants and Catholics is well-documented. Similarly, Sunni-Shia clashes are still continuing apace even today. If one wants to know most authentic details on the Christians sustained efforts of conversion in India,since ages one can look up the noted work of **Sitaram Goel (1921-2003), "History of Hindu-Christain Encounters (AD 304 to 1996)**. As a matter of fact, the Christian's sustained march in India has even led some people to observe that the Islamists are this regard, more open & honest in their intention of achieving conversions. It is learnt be that as it may, their efforts at vilifying Hinduism can indeed at times go to 'ridiculous' length, if one were to take it in lighter vein. To achieve their "target", they are stooping to any level, even through printed literature. The Christians have also been following various deceptive practices, such as, not changing their original Hindu names. How low they can go in this direction was proved a few years back in Kerala when they used to take Brahmin names to misguide the people. Briefly speaking, all these are through plain cheating and blackmail. One need not feel shy to state this even though we have very good friends in this community. Pope, John Paul II, during his last visit to New Delhi in November, 1999, had said, 'just as the first millennium saw the Cross firmly planted on the soil of Europe, and the second in that of America and Africa, the current millennium well witness a great harvest on the Asian subcontinent. The issue has indeed gained a threatening proportion and needs to be guarded against in a determined manner. May be the institutions like the Arya Samaj and Akhil Bharat Hindu Mahasabha, whose registered charter has the subject "to reclaim all those who left Hindu fold and welcome others into it, can lead the way to counter this burgeoning threat.

Invoke Women Power/'Stree Shakti'

Invoke Women Power/'Stree Shakti' in the language of **Swami Vivekananda**. After having had the benefit of exposure to the West (US), where women even in the latter half of the 19th century were so advanced and emancipated that Swamiji strongly felt the need for arousing "**Stree Shakti**" in India. He was clear that one of the primary reasons for India's backwardness was that "Stree Shakti" was disregarded here. He usedto openly say "**what can be achieved by five hundred men, can be achieved by five women only**. That is "Stree Shakti" which is still neglected in India". One needs only to recall the great historical role which Hindu mothers and sisters had played during invasions of barbaric freebooters by willingly sending their husbands, sons and brothers to the battlefield for defending the motherland. The inspirational role played by them during the freedom movement, especially in the earlier stages when the freedom fighters were being hounded out and labelled as 'terrorists' by the Britishers had indeed been exemplary. We learn the womenfolk in Bangladesh had also played a considerably significant role among the members of the Mukti Bahini in their India-supported independence movement. In basic or crude terms, when about 50% of the population comprises the women, how can any progress be achieved or any movement could succeed leaving them behind? That has been the lesson of history all over.

Hindus Need To Unite

Hindus Need To Unite: it may be proper at this stage to touch on this serious weakness among the Hindus. So has it been heard, the Hindu themselves are their worst enemies. However bitter, this is much nearer to the truth than generally believed. What the "Brahmanical tyranny" had started, the state has perpetuated by continuing with what had been envisaged as temporary measures in the Constitution for the uplift of the Scheduled Castes. The Mandal Commission had done the rest! Now, there are OBCs also. Who will break their heads to bring about the much-needed unification of the divided and sub-divided Hindu society? Today, the unification of Hindus has become a pressing necessity because of threats of conversion and distortions in history, discussed earlier. India, that is, **Bharatvarsh**, was one geographical entity as well as one spiritual entity.

It has, therefore, been repeatedly analysed and explained that the problem really lies with the Hindus themselves. So, has it been recently commented in the internet: "if 80% Hindus in the country could unite, what chances the Muslims would have in this country. Unfortunately, we have witnessed in the course of history Hindus letting down Hindus—rightfrom kings who remained divided, say, at the time of Alexander's invasion, to Mirzaffar, to Jaichand and to some big Hindu political leaders during the national freedom movement as well. The once mighty Hindu Kingdom stretching from Kandahar to Indonesia now reduced to its present stage, is just because the Hindus could never unite. So, the remaining India, the last bastion of the Hindus, may also soon fall apart-again-courtesy divided Hindus. One may not relish this but this has been harsh reality.

The attempt or the experiment of the **formation of the Hindu Dharma Acharya Mahasabha** is a great advance and must be fully supported and doggedly pusued. The major problem, it is understood, is that all Acharyas have their own fiefdom or followers and so the question often emerges who will take the lead on seat on the head table so to say.

Some thinkers,therefore, suggest the scholars of Hindu scriptures, religious preachers like the Dharmacharyas could perhaps take active interests in the political process for the sake of projecting the need for Hindus uniting to grow political strength and power that at times becomes imperative for self preservation or protection. Historically, the Jews can possibly offer an example to the Hindus in this regard.

Arouse The Hindu Middle Class Intelligentsia:

From all practical indications, the middle class intelligentsia among the Hindus have become impervious to any nationalist issues. Though this phenomenon calls for deeper sociological study of what can be called a malaise, laymen believe that the middle class intelligentsia earn enough to be happy and self-satisfied, and so are not bothered about what has been going around-be it social turmoil, economic down-turn or outbreak of communal tension or even terrorism. They feel confident they can "buy" peace and comfort for themselves. It is time to disabuse the mind of this set of people that form part of the whole. They will exist, if the nation survives. They will have to be reminded of the historic role this community had played in all countries all over the world in bringing about the desired changes in the society by providing leadership to all forward-looking movements, including "revolutions". It has been literally true in the case of India. It is incumbent to find out what has gone wrong with them. It is sadly observed they have gone dead here and hence the need to arouse them and shake them up. On feels like saying, it is necessary to "incite" them to save the Hindu community.

Tickle The Hindu Lawyers:

Here is another highly sensitive and significant community who can help the Hindus survive by taking recourse to legal remedies. The role of the eminent lawyers in the early stages of the national movement is written in golden letters. Where are their descendants? There are many, rather too many, brilliant lawyers among the Hindus, who can, without much difficulty and with little sacrifice, fight against the continued injustice and discriminations being perpetuated by the government against the Hindus, simply because they belong to the majority community. Examples galore. As members of the majority community, we can demand of them to play the role expected of this learned group to prevent or at least protest the planned aggression of the government against the poorest members of the majority community trapped in terminally ill rural areas and in utter discrimination by both the Central and State governments. Let the slogan for them be: "**Save The Brethren and Lead the Country Again**".

Appeal To The Hindu Youth

Following the law or process of evolution, which is indicative of positivism, the youth today are more knowledgeable and dynamic. But, unfortunately, because of adverse socio-economic conditions, lack of adequate or proper job opportunities according to their skills, this most vibrant section of the population is at times direction-less. They form the backbone of the nation and will continue to be so for all times to come. After all, they are the nation-builders. There is an imperative need to guide them and make them aware of their past history and present-day responsibilities in upholding what they have inherited from their forefathers. Their psyche has to be suitably turned to be both defenders and assertive of their inalienable rights. After all, the future of the country does depend on them, it actually belongs to them as well. Globally, India today has a headstart in the matter of youth-force with 15 to 35% of the population, which, we understand, will last for another about 30/40 years. So, we should take advantage of this accidental 'demographic potential' as a natural resource, as recently explained by **Dr. Subramanian Swamy**. The details of workable projects for them can be worked out on the ground. This youth potential can lead us to be the global power within a few decades or so,as earlier mentioned. Well, a leader has to emerge to lead them the right way. We may then perhaps again witness the phenomenon of another youth icon like Swami Vivekananda to arrive. Q. Has he already arrived?

It has, therefore, been beautifully said, "To divorce young Indians from the knowledge of their past is not only to alienate them from their own cultural soil but also to disinherit them from the sources that they could share with others for empowering humanity" (**Anindita Neogi Balshev**). And, we have no right to disinherit them!

Need To Expose Bitter Truth (Treachery of Jai Chandi Leaders)

The continued discrimination against the majority community by the power-that-be requires no elaboration but the full 'story' has to be quickly exposed. From the Sachar Committee Report, to the Ranganath Mishra Commission commendations (action taken report yet to be filed on the floor of the House) and continued government notifications, showering "benefits" on the minority community (now euphemistically called minority communities) at the cost of the poor Hindus is a full-blown conspiracy, which is on record. One may like to read all this in backdrop of the then Prime Minister of the country openly making the most unconstitutional statement, ever by any official, that the minorities have the first right to the natural resources of the country. That was in December 9, 2006, at the 52nd meeting of the National Development Council (http://www.pmindia.nic.in). The clarification to this announced on December 10, 2006, ((http://www.pmindia.gov.in/press-details.php) (?nodeid=516) hardly made any improvement. And, then a similar unconstitutional advisory from the formerUnion Home Minister to the State governments to ensure non-harassment of Muslim accused of terrorist charges, as if the same is not applicable to the accused from the minority community. Both these statements are still going unchallenged-thanks to vote bank politics of the country! Experts have studied these, collated them and have analysed them. The recently published pioneering work by **R.K. Ohri**&**J.P. Sharma**, titled "**The Majority Report**" gives a detailed examination of the monumental discrimination against the poorest of the poor Hindus by debarring their sons and daughters of any share in 20 million scholarships.

The **Sachar Committee**, which is constitutionally illegal under Art. 15 (1) of the Constitution, has also been challenged in the Delhi High Court, by a Delhi based '**Think Tank**', namely, the **Patriots' Forum** jointly with the Rashtriya Mukti Morcha. It has been clearly brought out that the recommendations made in the Sachar Committee Report were nothing but a political ploy for bestowing unmerited privileges on the Muslim community to buy their votes. In that sense, this Committee is nothing but mere continuum of the same age-old malaise to try to demolish the twin ideals of unity and integrity of the Indian people, as enunciated in the Preamble of the Constitution. Going through the details in this PIL (writ petition © 298/2008- Patriots' Forum Vs Union of India and others) will be great self-edification and so, is strongly recommended. It is learnt the Gujarat government has also very recently filed an affidavit before the Supreme Court, stating the Sachar Committee was unconstitutional. The affidavit pointed out the pre-matriculation minority scholarship programme, insisted upon by the Union Government on the basis of the Sachar Committee's recommendations, was arbitrary and discriminatory. The learned brothers and sisters in the legal profession can help immensely in this matter should they develop some inclination or show some commitment to the Hindu cause, so to say.

It is worth noting here the word 'minority' is not defined in the Indian Constitution. The two Articles in it—Articles 29 and 30—which mention the word 'minority read:

***Article 29*:Protection of interests of minorities**: "Any section of the citizens residing in the territory of India or any part of thereof having a distinct languages, script or culture of its own shall have the right to conserve them".

***Article 30*:Right of Minorities to establish and administer educational institutions**: "All minorities, whether based on religion or language, shall have the right to establish and administer educational institutions of their choice".

The editorial (November, 2013) in a noted magazine, titled **'Minority Rights' Meant for Hindus, but Hijacked by Muslims** (perhaps, more appropriately by the ruling establishment) has, therefore, rightly observed that there was **no concept of 'religious minority'** in the Indian Constitution. This had also been publicly announced a sometime back in a Seminar in Delhi by the revered saint late **Dayanand Saraswati** (of the present day). He had clearly announced that there could only be "ethnic minority but no religious minority at all. All religious and linguistic minorities have the right to establish **educational institutions**. The gravity of the deliberate misuse of executive authority can thus be well imagined.

One can further briefly allude here to the various other treatises on the clear and unmistaken misuse of Art 30 depriving the majority Hindu community of their fundamental rights vis-à-vis the 'minorities'. One is the governmental interference into the funds of the Hindu temples, now being fought in different courts of law, including the Supreme Court, and the other being many sections of Hindu sects trying to declare themselves non-Hindus and thus hoping to get the benefits and protection bestowed on the minorities. One stark but tragic example was the attempt by the Ramakrisha Math, founded by Swami Vivekananda, to get themselves recognized as a non-Hindu sect, thanks to the then CPM-led state government's brazen attempt to take control of all educational institutions initially agreed to by the Calcutta High Court but later rejected by the Supreme Court. The two significant references on these aspects and definitely worth reading are: (a) **Why this discrimination against the Hindus** by **J.G. Arora** in the Free Press Journal, Mumbai, August 26, 2005. (jgarora@vsnl.net). (b) **Making Lives Less Ordinary: Who is a Minority**: by **Sanjeev Nayyar**, May 4, 2007. (http://www.esamsanskriti.com/essay-chapters/making-lives-less-ordinary-who-is-a-minority-1.aspx).

Yet another case of almost constitutionally sanctioned discrimination under Article 30, against the Hindus is the disproportionate control by the minority Christian missionaries in some States over educational institutions. That, as has been beautifully explained, amounts to "egregious denial of empowerment and blunt religious discrimination" against the Hindus. (**Dr. Moorthy Muthuswamy** on a report on a workshop in **MIT, Harvard**, on 'India's Institutional Riot System' held on April 30, 2010, in his book **Religious**

Apartheid and Terror sponsorship in Modern India. Dr. Muthuswamy is a US-based nuclear physicist.

A friend with whom I had the privilege to discuss this aspect, advised that one could possibly do well to go into the details of this aspect in the records of the Constituent Assembly debates-a very valid suggestion but much beyond the scope of this study.

Fight To Prevent Corruption:

Corruption, to say the least, has become endemic and this cancer will have to be tackled first if one have to move forward.Theformer Prime Minister Rajiv Gandhi after a visit to a State had frankly admitted that from what he had seen on the ground, only about 10% of the sanctioned money was spent on bona-fide work, with the remaining 90% being siphoned off. No wonder India's place in the universal corruption index is so debasing or demeaning. There is no magic wand to remove it all of a sudden. It is basically a sociological phenomenon and will have to be studied accordingly as also be fought 'politically' and administratively. One point is certain, the problem has to be treated, if one were to use management terminology, in a 'top-down approach' but backed up by a bottom-up approach as well. Experience shows the rest then follows. Be that as it may, never before in the history of the country, corruption has been so pervasive at such high bureaucratic or political level as witnessed during the last ten years or so during the UPA I & II regime. Not many would perhaps be aware that apart from eating into the vitals of the country, extensive prevalence of such unchecked corruption tantamounts to grave risk to national security. This is a national problem but the majority community will have to take deeper interest in trying to eradicate or trying to lessening the impact of this virus, simply because it is "Hindusthan". May be the Lok Pal Bill will be of some help in this regard.

The relevance or significance of tackling this problem has been very well exemplified in the last Delhi elections. A politically young party (AAP) had role to power virtually on the plank of anti-corruption move, and in that sense, has perhaps set some precedence that will have long-term impact on the style of functioning of democracy in Indian hereafter.

Wake Up And Realise The Dangers: Demography Dynamics

Although this could have been the first item in this chain of thoughts, we kept it towards the end deliberately so as to impress upon the fellow citizens of the Hindu community **the gravity of the calamity** ahead or the reality part of it. This primarily relates to the almost irretrievable process of **fast-changing demographic composition of the country**, nay, even at the world stage. That demography is the mother of every democracy, has to be clearly understood and its implications duly appreciated. While experts in the West have awakened to the problem and have studied it, reaching a conclusion that the continent of Europe was likely to become an "**Eurabia**", the sad part of it is that India has yet to wake up to this often described as a 'demographic threat'. Even when faced with incontrovertible facts, responsible citizens including those having once occupied high posts, are unwilling to accept the unwelcome truth, turning a blind eye to this chapter of evolving history.

It will hurt fellow citizens to know there has so far been no authentic study of the long-term socio-political implications of demographic changes across India by the Indian government, much less to talk of setting up some dedicated centre to study that phenomenon in its entirety. The governments might be wrongly apprehending that such study could throw up the feeling this resulted indicated phenomenal growth of the Muslim population. But, demographic study is a sociological phenomenon without any communal overcome. Suffice it to state here that by internationally accepted human development indices, (such as, rate of death on birth, child mortality, average life expectancy at birth and degree of urbanisation), the Muslims in India are better off than their fellow members of the Hindu community. To add to this, the potential to grow more will be obvious from the revealed fact that the percentage of 0-6 old Muslims was much higher than the percentage in that same age group among the Hindus. The total decadal growth rate of the Muslims was also substantially higher than that of the Hindus in the period between 1991 to 2001. All this is according to the Census Report of the Government of India, 2001, and very significantly, minus the facts on the ground in the States of Assam and J & K. (Anyone wanting to know details on this issue, may see the relevant leaflet issued on the subject by the Patriots' Forum (www.

patriotsforum.org). A copy of it has been put in the appendix. Taking serious note of this phenomenon, some senior Hindu citizens have even started raising the question whether it was not time for the Hindus not strictly follow birth control measures.

In order to appreciate the full significance of the 'demographic threat', one needs to place it in the context of the strength of the growing Islamist fundamentalist forces all over the world and Al Qaeda's and now ISIS's special threat to India - thanks to their open and collusive activities in Pakistan being complemented by the increasing radicalization (rather talibanisation) of Islamist fundamentalists in Bangladesh and its impact on the State of West Bengal, literally encouraged by the State there, even though the said State, along with Assam & Bihar in particular, has been suffering the most from continued illegal migration from Bangladesh, a great existential threat by itself. We need to add the very recent threat exposed from the sudden burst of on October 2, 2014. Exposing the full play of the Jamaat from across Bangladesh, followed up by Al-Qaeda develop West Bengal as their Caliphate. Would you not also see this in the context of the open terrorist threat, often backed by the Pak ISI as well as the Pakistan government, coupled with unchallenged growth of the Indian Mujahideen, their open threat through the internet to the Hindus to get converted or face death and also increasing time-to-time exposure of the sleeper cells of the SIMI, and now also of the group known as the Peoples' Front of India in Kerala? This can be better appreciated from the fact that the Muslims in general and the jihadi elements in particular feel **scripturally obliged** to fight against and kill non-Muslims.

Indians must consider that when radicalization of Muslims is rapidly taking place worldwide, from the USA, Europe, Africa, West Asia, across South Asia (in Burma, Thailand and Sri Lanka) right upto Indonesia and the Philippines, can India escape this malignant virus of Islamofascism? This strategic issue must be brought out of closet by holding public discourses rather than relying on the lullabies sung by liberal leftists and self-anointed secularists.

Now, that we are in the period dominated what can be called "religious terrorism", indulged in by the biggest terror outfit ever, namely, the ISIS, a scourge to human civilisation. Al Queda, the parent major terrorist organisation, has now been reduced to second place. The Hindus must learn enough to appreciate the threat potential from these Islamic terror organisations. The Hindu parents must teach their children about the impeding threats lest they would blame the parents that knowing about the impending threats, they had not kept the children informed.

And, what is the estimate or understanding of the readers about the preparedness, ability and the dedication on the part of the government to face these security challenges, both from outside & inside the country? This is without touching on the Maoist threat that is considered by experts as of lesser significance or magnitude compared to that from the IM and SIMI, even though the former Prime Minister has described that as the biggest internal security threat.

An Observation

(It is worth pointing out at this stage another piece of very relevant information. The Muslim friends in India are far, far better off here, where they are in effect being treated as "sons-in-law", as some people rightly say, than in any Muslim majority or Islamic country, say, even in the Middle-East. Ask any Indian Muslim, he will virtually shudder to think of going out to these countries to settle down. The conditions of Muslim women there are still worse. Their religion lays down, we authentically learn, that women in Islam are like personal property of the man to whom she gets married and she is expected to procreate and multiply Muslims. Will this not explain why the growth rate of the Muslims both in India & other countries is going up and up? To add to that, they are also forbidden to go out for joining any service to earn their livelihood. In the Middle-East countries, some enlightened Muslim ladies, exposed to education and western culture, are waking up and protesting. A Saudi princess has written a book, exposing multiple tribulations and torture from the family with reference to her personal life. One can also add to this the specific genetic problem in the Muslim community, arising out of their in-built and preferred system of in-breeding.)

Taking the facts stated in '**Expose The Truth**' and "**Know And Realise The Dangers**", a keen observer of the scene went to the extent of opining that it was good the country (India) had been partitioned. It has been a blessing in disguise. Otherwise, we the Hindus would have been by now living in a Muslim-majority country with easily imaginable consequences. We leave it to the readers to assess this observation on their own.

Know Facts About Fast-paced Communal Divide

It is common knowledge among the law and order functionaries of both the Central and State Governments as also the Election Commission that areas having 20% to 25% or more of Muslim population are taken to be communally sensitive and accordingly, appropriate measures are taken to prevent communal conflagration in those areas. Both facts and statistical analysis support this. According to a study, in circulation on the internet, it has been factually established that over 75% of the communal riots in India have been caused by the Muslims. Deeper study may show the said percentage to be still higher. Incidentally, all the seven days in a week, the largest incidence of communal riots happen on Friday. Before starting a witch-hunt against Hindus, the government must analyse and understand why communal violence erupts mostly on Fridays—not only in India, but across the world. This aspect needs to be debated publicly.

Learn Some Lessons From Muzaffarnagar Riots

The Hindu-Muslim riots (August-September, 2013) in Muzaffarnagar (UP) was, in the above context, a clear dress-rehearsal for the shape of things to come on the communal front all over the country. According to experts, this was a dry-run for gaining supremacy on the Gangetic plane, the cradle of the Indic civilization. Perhaps, the count-down has begun. The wild rumours about the extent of armed preparation (including reported use of AK-47 rifles during Muzaffarnagar riots) by the Muslims in the region will be indicative of the deeper plan to carve out the "Mughalistan" of the dreams of jihadi storm-troopers. The large number of ISI-sponsored sleeper cells in the Hindi heartland has been known since long. Similarly, the "no-go" areas for the police in this entire region have also been increasing over the years. There thus emerges a distinct need for the authorities for recalibrating the strategy to maintain internal security in the area and for the Hindus to acquaint themselves with the ground realities and the Islamic mind. One can add to this the apparent discriminatory attitude of the local police against the Hindus in the matter of either not listening to their complaints of large scale incidence of "love jihad", i.e., to conquer the world through what that braveheart lady scholar late **Oriana Fallaci** described as the battle of the womb. To these threats must be added the looming fear of large number of arrests of the Hindus on trumped up charges! The ground situation in many parts of India on this front, according to security analysts, has become somewhat reminiscent of the communal frenzy of the pre-partition days. This assessment will have to be taken seriously and necessary preemptive thoughts and preparations worked out to maintain and uphold the territorial integrity of the nation.

Know The Muslim Mind

One will at this stage do best to study the analysis, done in his book on "**Slavery, Terrorism and Islam: The Historic Riots and Contemporary Threat**", by the famous Dutch author **Peter Hammond**, of the psychology and behaviour-pattern of the Muslim community world over. His readings are rather pointed. When the Muslim community is around 2% of the total population, they "begin proselytising", and from 5% onwards, they "exercise inordinate influence in proportion to their percentage of the population". At this point, they will work to get the ruling government to allow them to rule themselves (within their ghettos) under Sharia law, that is, the Islamic law. At 10%, they tend to increase lawlessness as a means of complaint about their conditions (India with 13.4% at that point of time, fell into this group). At their reaching 20%, "nations can expect hair-trigger rioting, jihad militia formations, sporadic killings and the burning of Churches & synagogues, etc". One can add Hindu temples, etc. in this category. This in effect means **the Muslim friends know how to make their numbers**

count. The Hindus with about 80% of the population miserably fail in this respect. It may also be noted that the Muslim friends in India make too much of the so-called 'victimhood' theory by making much of even very minor incidents. All these will have to be read in the backdrop of tremendous amount of sophistry in the armoury of those who indulge in these kinds of activities. This also falls in line with the simple fact that the Muslims feel "scripturally bound" to fight against all non-Muslims, as mentioned earlier.

Fight the Prevention of Communal Violence Bill If Raised Again

It is a different matter that despite this knowledge-bank with all concerned, the last UPA II Government was keen on bringing up the "Prevention of Communal and Targeted Violence Bill (PCTV), proposed by NAC (National Advisory Council, chaired by Sonia Gandhi). The Bill was patently anti-Hindu and based on the presumption of guilt of the majority community, perhaps primarily because ultimately the minority community, found to be providing the provocation on most of the occasions, suffers more casualty. On the face of it, this proposed Bill was worse than the IMDT Act earlier imposed on Assam to protect Bangladeshi Muslim immigrants there. The IMDT Act has since been declared null & void by the Supreme Court. The "obnoxious" PCTV Bill, has also fortunately gone to the cold storage.

Questioning the Authorities Promoting Islam/Muslim Cause

It is significant to recall the NDA Government had immediately after the 9/11/2001, banned **The Islamic Student Movement of India** (SIMI), now converted to Indian Mujahideen, for being openly anti-Indian and vowing allegiance to the Al Qaeda leader Bin Laden. Sonia Gandhi and her party had, inside the House, vigorously opposed (2001 itself) this ban. And, then when the UPA government came to power, they allowed the ban on SIMI to lapse in 2005. It so happened the Supreme Court directed the government to re-impose this ban, which was done in 2006. The typical anti-Hindu attitude of Rahul Gandhi, manifested when he said that Hindu communalism/organizations were more dangerous than Muslim communalism. Also, Salman Khursid, then MP, was the advocate for the SIMI in courts. All these are on record. Does anyone require any external enemy with such attitude and activity of "Indian nationals"?

Need To Exercise Franchise

This important constitutional duty is not often performed by a good number of Hindus. Voting is voluntary but its full use must be made in a democratic form of government. The Hindus needed to ensure to bring to power those who will pledge to protect the Indic civilization, uphold the Vedic values so as to be able to speak from a position of strength, the strength of numbers. A Muslim friend was frank enough to state that the Muslims vote enbloc because of fear psychosis-the fear of being neglected or denied what they presume as their rights. The same fear psychosis has to be built among the Hindus more urgently because the fear, the danger they face (but the majority among them not yet realizing) is one of extinction, both in number and culturally, rather civilisationally. The small discussion earlier on the demographic factor would have clearly brought out that aspect. What the almost 1000 years of Muslim rule could not do to India, will be achieved on the ground by the force of Islamic fundamentalists then they could outnumber the Hindus in this Hindusthan. So there is as an urgent need for the Hindus to consolidate politically as well and to learn "bloc voting", as the Muslim friends do.

Hindus Must Draft and Present a Charter of Demands

(**To be done by a Citizens' Body**, comprising both Hindus and non-Muslims alike: by residents of Hindustan. The emphasis is on Hindus as the responsibility lies on the shoulders of the majority community).

- **Uniform Civil Code**, as provided in the Constitution;
- **Withdrawal/Scrapping of Art. 370,** which is a "temporary" provision and according to some legal luminary, can be done ……… way with by an executive order. The demand for a debate on this issue has already been raised and would require to be pursued;

- **Vigorous Educational Reforms**-in the words of Swami Vivekananda, we need education that not only bestows knowledge but also helps character formation. Introduce Vedic Sanatan Dharma in mainstream academic curricula and bring in of Sanskrit because these are needed for saying prayers.
- **Scrapping of All Reservations,** which were also temporary provisions but being maintained for political purposes (earlier discussed);
- **Restoration of Historic Hindu Temples,** such as, Ram Mandir, and the temples at Mathura and Kashi (Varanasi). It is known the Muslims do not hesitate to bring down masjids or mosques in Islamic countries when needed. This is not any communal demand. This is only reclaiming legitimate rights, as established by history and archaeological and scientific researches. The demand for scrapping of the proposed Ram Setu Project also falls in this category;
- **Renaming of India as Hindusthan**/Bharatvarsh or Bharat Mata, as Swami Vivekananda used to address;
- **National Slogan and Mode of First Address: Vandemataram** (on which the entire freedom movement had started and fought) or "**Jai Hind**", coined by Netaji Subhash Chandra Bose.

(Comments: All these are possible under the existing administrative and legal system. In other words, most of these are easily implementable and do not involve financial investments. All that is needed is to express political desire/decision and administrative will.

We strongly believe the vast majority of the Hindus (and many Muslim friends also) are nationalists at heart. They have to think how to realise these demands. Let us remember silence is not always golden. We will have to make our voice heard. One practical way would be to create a strong public opinion, which is of great value in a democracy. A common man's view is patriotism is nationalism and so let all of us be true patriots. In the words of **Swami Vivekananda, "Be a fierce patriot"**. And, getting back to thinking, we must cultivate the habit of thinking. It is the power of thinking that leads to the growth of ideas. And, it is ideas that make history. We in the present generation and our children will have to rewrite the history in order to put back the country to its past glory and on top of the comity of nations, as envisaged by Swami Vivekananda.

What Does the Future Hold for the Nation (read the Hindus)?

Somewhat summarising , let us at this stage take a bird's eye view of what one can see lying ahead of us. With the inexorable march of the socio-economic phenomenon of demography, clearly indicating the high growth rate of the Muslim population in India, with still more potential to grow on account of much larger proportion of co-horts in 0-6 years age group), it will be worthwhile to briefly recount the **negative factors** first:

Identifying and Eradicating Negative Factors Afflicting Hindu Society.

- The somnambulant Hindu community at large and its so-called leadership in particular are either deliberately indifferent to the demographic issue or are incapable of appreciating its significance, a condition described by experts as "**Hindus Are Under Siege**". Some scholars call it a typical case of **'intellectual abdication' of their responsibility**;
- The 'virtual death' of the Hindu middle-class intelligentsia; their inertia and indifference to the national cause.
- Absence of any religious or cultural training for the Hindus at any level;
- Inadequate teaching of Indian history and culture;
- Lack of pride among the Hindus cutting across all sections, about their past glory and achievements;
- Give up excessive emphasis on the spirit of tolerance, assimilation and synthesis verging on 'escapism' by ignoring the ethos of valour quotient prescribed for Hindus, deeply reflected in the Shastras and practised on the ground in the past;
- Surging but rudderless or direction-less youth community of the Hindus;
- Severely divided and subdivided Hindu society with no effective or possible improvement in sight;
- Continuing discrimination against the majority community by the government, going unopposed, that is, the Hindu lawyers, barring a very few exceptions, not being moved whatsoever–an unpardonable failure to play their due role.

Conquering The Chaos:

We will here like to share with the readers what the former **Chairman of Microsoft India, Ravi Venkatasen**, the author of "**Conquering The Chaos! Win in India, Win Everywhere**", had said, "Indians will have to reclaim their country. *That means becoming responsible and truly engaged citizens. They will have to start following the law even when there are few consequences for breaking it. They will have to vote in election and pay taxes instead of bribes. They will have to get out on the streets to protest publicly and vigorously against injustices - not just once, when some horrible scandal moves them, but consistently. They have to donate money and time to strengthen NGOs and volunteer organisations. Unless honest and patriotic leaders replace the cynics and crooks, efforts to change the system will never gain sufficient momentum. It is no longer appropriate for Indians to ignore the chaos around them. Their disengagement is producing a dysfunctional and unliveable society. If they do not conquer the chaos, chaos will conquer India.*"

Know And Realise The Dangers:

(Applicable to the nation as a whole and to the Hindus in particular whether a believer or an atheist because they yet now constitute the majority in number)

Internal:

- Lackof governance with no adequate accountability

– all plans and schemes come to naught for total failure of their implementation;

- Tales of corruption – the country has never before gone through such phase of corruption, thoroughly eating in to the vitals of the administration;
- Intensive politico – bureaucratic and criminal nexus, bringing to the fore the criminal elements, a sure route to administrative breakdown;
- Growing erosion of faith in weakened, inadequate and thoroughly politicized administration, especially the police forces, at all levels – a dangerous portent for all-round anarchy;
- Despite being adequately identified, the Maoist movement continued to pose a serious threat, with reasonable apprehension of foreign assistance and support from the Indian Mujahideen, especially in terms of augmenting their armoury;
- Absence of any practical and coordinated policy or action in public view to tackle or minimize the terrorist menace, posed by Pak-sponsored outfits;
- Lack of cohesion and growing distrust between the Centre and the States, leading to growth of fissiparous tendencies, with possibilities of seriously threatening the federal structure of the Constitution/the country;
- Increasing deterioration of the overall communal temper in the country, with the Muzffarnagar riots (August, 2013) exposing the ground realities and future portents;
- Increasing spread and influence of the IM and SIMI and now the ISIS and Al Qaeda, with potential for

further growth with external guidance and support and yet not looking to be being treated seriously.

External:

- No 'true' friends among the nations encircling India, i.e., neighbourhood countries – a story of losing friends continuously, e.g., Bangladesh, Nepal and Sri Lanka;
- Continuing security threats of different magnitude both from the West and the East, especially after the US withdrawal from Afghanistan;
- Pakistan government not in control of the jihadi forces, not even sure of keeping the Afghan jihadi's separate from the Kashmiri jihadi groups;
- Pak Army & ISI continuing their philosophy of "thousand cuts" & dismembering India;
- Illegal migration from Bangladesh continuing-a great existentialist threat by itself;
- Islamic fundamentalist forces gaining more and more ground within Pakistan, spreading Wahabbism, as also in Bangladesh, with their impact on Indian Muslims.
- Continued rise in the number of people steeped in jihadi philosophy, coming out of the madrassas, often described as "hate factories";
- Practical 'war' between India and Pakistan (though not admitted by either side) going on since long along the LOC in the name of infiltrations, exposing chinks in national defence policy;
- Virtually losing 'control' over the Indian Ocean, considered "India's backwaters" in the past;

- China playing on India's weakness on the international border;
- No serious or material help from either US or Russia;

Need to Restrategise Hindu Approach

Having taken brief note of the negative factors and the points of danger, both internal and external, it will be relevant to note what strategy the Hindus need to adopt to counter these challenges. Following our own Kautilya or the Chinese war-philosopher Sun Tsu, earlier referred to, it is imperative in any confrontation, say, the war, to know the enemy as well. In the case of our struggle to save the Indian civilisational ethos, which primarily speaks of assimilation and tolerance, the dangers have already been identified. The Muslims derive their strength from scriptural dictation that clearly stipulates deception, and in these days of technology, they are also highly sophisticated and tech-savvy. This situation has to be met by restrategising our approach, for the sake of protecting 'dharma'. Lord Krishna was prepared to break his vow of not taking up arms in the war in order to uphold 'dharma'. The Hindus will have to work out equally practical, sophisticated and need-based technology and material strength to fight off the enemy, so to say. Down the line in history, as already pointed out, the Hindus had been oppressed, tortured and what not, but they remained defiant and never capitulated either mentally or spiritually. That fighting morale will have to be kept up.

Conclusion

Ray of Hope:

In its chequened history, India had once grown and developed a civilization which has stood the test of time. It suffered foreign incursions, loot, plunder, murder on unprecedented scale. Then, the country suffered foreign rule, both Muslim and British. The 1000- year Muslim rule could not affect the civilisational ethos; may be they were unable to break the Hindu valour and moral courage. But, the Britishers (Lord Macaulay leading the way) divined and understood the source of resilience of the Indian culture and hence seriously attacked and changed the basic educational system of the country. It produced both positive and negative results. The positive aspect is often forgotten. The introduction of the western education resulted in the flowering of what is called the "**Bengal Renaissance**", the intellectual precursor of the Indian national movement. It produced among others men like Rammohan Roy and Swami Vivekananda. Confining to Swami Vivekananda, the man who changed for ever the religious discourse in the world and put India/ Hinduism on the world stage, **C. Rajagopalachari** had said, ***'Swami Vivekananda saved Hindustan and saved India. But for him, we would have lost our religion and would not have gained our freedom"***. In the language of Netaji Subhash Chandra Bose, ***"The foundation of the present freedom movement owes its origin to Swamiji's message. If India is to be free, it cannot be***

a land of specially of Hinduism or of Islam-it must be one united land of different religious communities inspired by the ideal of nationalism". Netaji Subhas Chandra Bose had also said. Indians must accept whole-heartedly the gospel of harmony of religions which is the gospel of Rama-Krishna-Vivekananda". That was the catholicity of the Hindu monk, of Hindu civilisation.

Whether this assessment holds or will hold good in today's environment of total distrust between the two communities is a matter of perception or debate. In fact, the politically-shunned debate has already started. Referring to a write-up "The Clutches of Communal Frenzy" in The Statesman by one Firoz Bakht Ahmed (September 8, 2013) and a panel discussion organised by The Statesman on September 16, 2013, on **Who's Afraid of a Hindu Rashtra**", an informed reader rebutted in the "Letters to the Editor" column, "Communal harmony between Hindus and Muslims is nothing short of a utopian dream given the lack of spiritual insight and vision of both communities to realize the gulf of difference in the two totally distinct religious ideologies of the Upanishad and the Quran". "How can Hinduism and Islam run on parallel lines socially, according to Ahmed, unless there is a common ground? Islam divides mankind along the lines of mumin (believer) and Kafir (non-believer). Unless there is a humanistic approach, the communal divide (between the Hindus and Muslims) will persist. Quite contrary to the theology of tolerance and peace prescribed in the Upanishads, the Quran believes in one God - the Allah and decimation of all other faiths. Thedemarcation between monotheism and polytheism is evident, the Hindus belonging to the latter category". This conundrum has remained for centuries and will perhaps remain unresolved. A debate has been going ground, mostly in the West, whether Islam is a religion at all or is a pure political strategy only to gain power over the entire world.

Be that as it may, we strongly believe Swami Vivekananda, the destiny's child, still remains the only hope before the beleaguered nation. Much in tune with the Indian civilisational ethos, Swamiji in his final message at Chicago on September 27, 1893, had underlined: 'Upon the banner of every religion will soon be written, in spite of resistance: Help and Not Fight,"Assimilation and not Destruction', "Harmony and Peace and not Dissension".

Can we achieve this in the backdrop of what we have attempted to outline in this small book? All Hindus, irrespective of their origin, education, location, level of education and local culture, must help achieve that Millennium. In the famous words of Swamiji, "Arise and Awake And Not Stop Till The Goal Is Reached" and then let us act and learn to sacrifice a bit for the sake of the Motherland. We had been in the past conquered physically (never culturally) but we had rebounded, again overrun and yet again recovered. That is, we, the Hindus of Hindusthan or Bharatvarsh, had never capitulated, and we do hope we will not. Our deep faith in the forces of the past history have kept us going. So, let our resolve or take a "sankalpa" to defend our motherland and 'dharma' and be as strong and resolute, as in the unforgettable lines of Tagore:

"If they answer not to thy call, walk alone
If they are afraid and cower mutely facing the wall,
O thou unlucky one,
open thy mind and speak out alone.
If they turn away, and desert you when crossing the wilderness,
O thou unlucky one,
trample the thorns under thy tread,
and along the blood-lined track travel alone.
If they do not hold up the light when the night is troubled with storm,
O thou unlucky one,
with the thunder flame of pain ignite thy own heart,
and let it burn alone."

I humbly feel and advise the readers that they will be immensely benefitted by going through, in addition to **The Majority Report**, mentioned in this note:

- The most classical (the first such bold attempt) book on the subject, "**The Long March of Islam**", by **Shri R.K. Ohri**, and
- '**Wake Up or Perish**, (a civilisational challenge to Hindu Identity), published in April 2013, by **Shri Madhu Deolkar**.

IT IS A SIN TO BE A HINDU IN INDIA

- The story goes a foreigner, on return to his country, was asked how did he find the Indians. With a look of surprise on his face, he replied he had not found any Indians in India. They were either Punjabis, Rajasthanis, Biharis, Tamilians, Bengalis, etc.
- Similarly, if one would ask who are the Hindus in India, the obvious answer will be: there are no Hindus in India (no longer known as Bharatbarsha). They are either upper caste Brahmins, Kayasthas, et all, or, Scheduled Castes, Scheduled Tribes, Backward Castes, et all and Muslims, Christians, Buddhist, Sikhs, et all.
- To cap it all, the highest court of the land has, in its wisdom, characteristically declared that Hinduism is a way of life, i.e., not a religion, creating confusion among the 'believers'.
- So, we all have to find out to which categories of so-called Indians, the religious scriptures like the Upanishads, the Vedas and religious books like Ramayana, Mahabharta, Gita, et all, belong to.
- For Muslims, Islamic studies, such as, the Koran, etc are being taught in Madrasas & some specific Muslim Institutes, Universities and Study or Cultural Centers. Christians have their own

Missionary Centres and Churches to teach them the tenets the trends of Christianity.

- For those multitude of about 80% of the population, who go by the generic terminology of Hindus, there is only one dedicated Hindu University at Banaras.
- Religion, as such, is not taught in schools & colleges in India because that will, it is argued, go against the Directive Principles of the present-day Indian Constitution, amended to be known as 'Secular', an expression not there in the original Constitution made by those forefathers, who in their wisdom, deliberately did not make any misuse or misinterpretation of the term "Secular", whose dictionary meaning is : "concerned with affairs of the world; not spiritual or sacred" (Oxford Dictionary).
- A citizen of India has the Fundamental Right of Freedom of Religion. So, if you declare yourself a Muslim, you can justifiably be known as secular. If you declare yourself as a Christian, you can justifiably be a secular individual too. But, if you proclaim yourself as a Hindu or as a Hindu nationalist, you are suspected to be or presumed to be communal.
- The Prime Minister of India had publicly pronounced that the minorities in India (a term not defined in the Indian Constitution but meant to cover the followers of Islam till its meaning has recently been expanded to include other communities, smaller in number, such as, Sikhs, Jains, Buddhists, Christians and Parsis) will have

the first right to natural resources of the nation. It is the most unconstitutional statement made ever by any government official or politician at any level, much less to talk about at the level of the Prime Minister and that too by such a universally acclaimed and learned economist Prime Minister Manmohan Singh. Interestingly, such an egregious statement is yet going unchallenged, even by the so-called pro Hindu political party like the BJP.

- The 'trump card' with the Government of India to work ceaselessly towards 'improving' the lot of the Muslims (though they are not disadvantaged by the universally accepted four very important human development indices) is the Sachar Committee Report – a Committee that is unconstitutional under Art. 15 of the secular Constitution of India and has been so challenged at the Delhi High Court six years back. The finding of the now famous Sachar Committee Report has also been publicly rebutted as late as in October, 2011, at a Seminar organized by the United Nations Development Programme (UNDP) and India's Planning Commission in New Delhi.
- This action of the Central Government inspired many State governments to join the race to bestow similar or other benefits to non-Hindus i.e., the minorities (mainly, the Muslims), the States of UP, Bihar and West Bengal leading the show. Most of these, if not all, measures are unconstitutional but these are going unchallenged. Art 15 (1) of the Indian Constitution stipulates: the State shall

not discriminate against any citizen on grounds of religion, caste, sex, place of birth or any of them. The famous press statement of the former Minister for Minority Affairs (Salman Khurshid) made on May 12, 2012, is a landmark, spelling out the details of benefits and welfare measures till then conferred on the minority communities (available on the internet: http//: indiacurrentaffairs.org/ financial-and-physical-achievements-of- ministry-of-minorityaffairs) is worth remembering in this connection. The purpose of referring to these achievements of the Central government is to underscore that the vast majority of Hindus are deprived of the munificence from the government. This hurts more the Hindus in the rural areas, the poorest and most underprivileged lot in the country, who constitute the vast multitude of the Indian population. They are unaware of such blatant discrimination against them simply because they are Hindus, i.e., being discriminated against on ground of religion in stark violation of the provisions of the Indian Constitution, just quoted above.

- Even though the Govt. is yet to submit 'action taken' report on the Ranganath Mishra Commission Report, again blatantly recommending concessions to the Muslims, many State government have started implementing its recommendations as well.
- The readers may at this stage like to acquaint themselves with the details spelt out by Salman Khurshid of the government's achievements in

favour of the Muslim/minority communities. Nothing more will perhaps be required to justify the title of the paper that it is a sin to be Hindus in India. If some one will be interested to know more details of deliberate deprivation of the Hindus by the governments in the Centre and States, these could be directly obtained from scholars like Shri R.K. Ohri (ram.ohri.ohri@gmail.com) and Shri J.P. Sharma (sharmjp@gmail.com) as also the website (www.opgupta.org). Interestingly, the details of 16 websites providing information about the various free scholarship, being granted to the Muslims have also been beautifully put in the website of the Kerala-based Islamist Group, Popular Front of India (PFI): http://popularfrontofindia.com/pp/story/scholarships-indian-muslims).

- Yet another new technique is being displayed by the Central Government. Muslims accused in terror-related cases (the vast majority of the accused and arrested in connection with terrorist cases in India) are being screened and being allowed to go scot-free even when the cases are investigation. While, on the other hand, Hindu activists arrested only on suspicion are being more and more harassed. The general press highlights the governments' "benevolent" attitude towards Muslim suspects but are mute observers in respect of what is clear and deliberate harassment because he or she-suspect is a Hindu. We do hope we do not need to provide the details of such cases.
- Incidentally, the fund for all these privileged groups comes from taxes paid mostly by the hapless

Hindus, who 'incidentally' still form the majority community in India.

- It will not be incorrect to highlight at the end that all that has been shared here is fact & fact alone. No interpretation has been added---- whether to take or not to take this on the face value is the readers' choice.
- A legitimate question arises here: how or why the Hindus are not protesting against such open and huge discriminations against them. No clear answer is perhaps available. In any case, that will need a detailed study and an in-depth analysis of typical Hindu characteristics. We will leave it for another day.

(Note: Much of the information catered in the Note is general knowledge. The rest is as learnt from established scholars mentioned in the Note. I take this opportunity to sincerely acknowledge my debt to them publicly.)

Tribute To Rishi Bankim Chandra

"There were many Rishis of old, the inspired creators of thoughts and civilisation, not to be repeated among degenerate in these distressful days. Ours is the eternal land of the eternal people and eternal religion, whose strength, greatness, holiness may be overclothed but never, even for a moment utterly ceasing. The hero, the Rishi, the saint are the natural fruits of our Indian soil; and there has been no age, in which they have not been born. Among the Rishis of the late age, we have at least realised that we must include the name of the man, who gave us the reviving mantra, which is creating a new India with that mantra,"Bande Mataram". He is none other than Rishi Bankim Chandra.

Rishi Auorvindo